BUILDING A
BUSINESS

By:

Deborah Siegel

Copyright 2015 by Content Arcade Publishing - All rights reserved.

This document is geared towards providing exact and reliable information in regards to the topic and issue covered. The publication is sold with the idea that the publisher is not required to render accounting, officially permitted, or otherwise, qualified services. If advice is necessary, legal or professional, a practiced individual in the profession should be ordered.

- From a Declaration of Principles which was accepted and approved equally by a Committee of the American Bar Association and a Committee of Publishers and Associations.

In no way is it legal to reproduce, duplicate, or transmit any part of this document in either electronic means or in printed format. Recording of this publication is strictly prohibited and any storage of this document is not allowed unless with written permission from the publisher. All rights reserved.

The information provided herein is stated to be truthful and consistent, in that any liability, in terms of inattention or otherwise, by any usage or abuse of any policies, processes, or directions contained within is the solitary and utter responsibility of the recipient reader. Under no circumstances will any legal responsibility or blame be held against the publisher for any reparation, damages, or monetary loss due to the information herein, either directly or indirectly.

Respective authors own all copyrights not held by the publisher.

The information herein is offered for informational purposes solely, and is universal as so. The presentation of the information is without contract or any type of guarantee assurance.

The trademarks that are used are without any consent, and the publication of the trademark is without permission or backing by the trademark owner. All trademarks and brands within this book are for clarifying purposes only and are the owned by the owners themselves, not affiliated with this document.

Table of Contents

INTRODUCTION

Do you find being your own boss appealing?

Who doesn't—at first, that is. I wish I had a dollar for every time I've heard a young hopeful say they wished they could start a business so they wouldn't have to answer to anyone else. Newsflash, having your own business doesn't mean you don't have to answer to anybody. Truth is, you'll probably have hundreds of bosses, and they'll all want something from you. The best entrepreneurs consider every customer to be their boss. Entrepreneurs know that most employees and customers have the upper hand, with employment and consumers laws designed to protect them from unfair business practices and unjust employment requirements. You'll be your own boss, alright—just behind your accountant, the government, and everybody else looking for a handout.

Do you like the idea of socializing with all those with whom you work?

Let's talk truth here, shall we? Few employees want to socialize with their boss. They don't mind a little chat at work every so often, but even that can be accompanied by fear that you've paid them a visit to increase their workload or complain about their performance. If there is a rare employee who seeks you out for social hour, you'll be spending most of the evening wondering if they're trying to butter you up or tap you for trade secrets. Either way, there's usually minimal enjoyment when socializing with your employees. It's difficult for them to complain about the boss to you when you ARE the boss.

Do you dream of making the big bucks?

That may be the case as you get farther on down the road, but in the beginning you'll resemble a circus elephant—you'll carry the show and work for peanuts. If you are currently an employee at the high end of your employment pay scale, you may want to rethink the whole entrepreneurial thing. It's difficult to give up a big paycheck for the idea of a business that will require longer hours, less pay, and no vacations for the first few years. There is rarely instant gratification when building a business.

So, you want to name your own hours, right?

Mistake! Huge mistake, unless the hours you absolutely love are from opening to close. Most business owners are the first to arrive and the last to leave six to seven days a week. However, it doesn't stop there. On the rare occasion they get to take a day off, they usually spend it at home catching up on paperwork. Few new entrepreneurs can afford the luxury of having an accountant, multiple managers, and 100 percent dependable staff to handle all things all hours.

Do you believe you have a business idea that is a guaranteed success?

Hate to break it to you, but there is no such thing! When you enter into business, there is no guarantee for success. No matter how many are raking in the dough in your chosen industry, this means very little when predicting your possibilities. Everybody is different and so are their companies, even when they are in a related industry. About the only guarantee you can expect is that you have some pretty heavy duty surprises coming your way that you have NOT prepared for, and they're guaranteed to change the course of your business.

Do you still want to build a business, knowing that 8 out of 10 small businesses fail within the first three years? If so, the best we can hope for is to help you prepare to be the boss of you. Do yourself a favor, though, resist the temptation to jump in before cautiously sticking a toefirst to test the water. Good idea--let this book be your test toe.

Chapter One—Ground Level Looking Up

A great thing about starting at ground level, you've got nowhere to go but up. For time's sake, let's assume you already have a field, product, or service in mind for your first business. You also have any additional training or education your endeavor requires, or you've been apprenticing for quite some time and now feel ready to take the helm. If you've come this far, it would probably also be safe to say that you've obtained or are applying for your business licenses and your corporate documents. Whew! That's over and you're ready to go fast!

Back up and take a breath. Chances are your business ideas are not original, and nobody is going to steal your thunder if you take just a little while longer in this initial start-up phase. There are a few little things to do that could have a big impact on your success. One of those things is to talk to others who already own a business in your chosen field. If possible, visit their business and shadow them for a day. It promises to be an eye-opening experience. You'll see things and learn things you never thought of when dreaming about opening your business. If nothing else, it could show you what you don't want to do as you open your doors.

Next, when you find a location or store front that looks promising, talk to other tenants leasing from the same landlord. Tell them of your plans and ask them the terms of their lease. People are happy to inform you of the good, the bad, and the ugly. My friend saved thousands because he took the time to ask his neighboring tenant about the terms of his lease. He had never had a store front before, and had no idea about how to negotiate or what special offerings he could expect. He also learned about some high dollar deposits that were required from the city before opening. The other tenant told him he had refused to pay the city the deposit they asked, and so they simply waived it and approved his occupancy anyway. Knowing this, my friend put $10,000 back into his pocket that would have been paid in deposits plus $57,000 in paid build-outs that was later applied to some other unexpected expenses.

There are many questions to ask your future landlord, but I call the following ones the Safety Six—if your landlord answers no to all six, run for safety.

1. Will the landlord pay for build-outs? Build-outs include any special additions

to the property that are required to operate your business. You might need extra plumbing, electricity, a lowered ceiling, additional walls or rooms, an additional bathroom, etc...

2. Will the landlord give four to six months free lease on the front end to give you an opportunity to build your business? Most will do this and tack those months onto the end of the lease.

3. Has the landlord disclosed all restrictions of the leased space? One of my friends planned on opening a small pet supply store, to include a grooming shop and boarding facility down the road as additional revenue sources. She opened the store, but learned twelve months later when planning to build her boarding facility that there were restrictions that did not allow that type

of business to be conducted on the premises.

4. Has the landlord included signage space that can clearly been seen from the main highway? Many of the smaller strip centers are constructed with empty pads in front. The landlord plans to lease these pads to future tenants after the main center is occupied. You'll just want to make sure future plans do not obstruct the view of your store's sign.

5. Will your landlord promise not to lease to another business providing the same service or product as you plan to in your business? If the landlord will not give you exclusive rights with your business, look elsewhere.

Setting a budget is also essential in the initial phase of your planning. This is when you can and should exaggerate the figures. When planning your budget, estimate your expenses high and your income low. This will give you a little wiggle room during the first few months of business when you may have a lot of leftover cost at the end of your customers for the month. There's nothing like opening a business that looks spectacular and is talked about by many as the best in the business. However, make sure all the cash you are putting out to be remarkable is a solid investment. If this is your first business, it's always better to keep a low overhead to ensure a successful beginning. Streamlining your start-up doesn't mean that you have to pinch pennies forever—just until you have a clear vision of your profit and loss. Putting your money back into the business is a great practice, but first you've got to make sure you have the money.

Speaking of money, if your business is to provide a service, it's time you figured out what the proper pricing will be for that service. Take a look at your competition; what do they charge for similar services? Will your pricing be higher? Will you be providing added value to your customers? If so, make sure they realize what that added value is so they won't simply think you're pricing yourself out of the market. You may mistakenly think that undercutting your competition would be a good way to attract consumers. Before you are tempted to take the prices to an all-time low, think about what kind of customer you want to attract. If it is the bargain shopper, and there's nothing wrong with that, then low, low prices may be the way to go. However, if you want your reputation to be built on service and high quality, those things will cost you more money that will need to be passed on to your customers or come out of your pocket.

One thing you can count on when building your business, is that you'll never have enough. There is never enough money, enough time, or enough customers. The amount of time you have to get everything done and the number of customers you get walking through your doors are somewhat out of your control. What you can control at ground level is how much money you have put aside for your initial start-up. Unfortunately, it usually takes three to four times more than you budgeted to begin your business. Raising prices to cover unexpected expenses will not give you the desired results of putting more money in your pocket. Once you've set prices, it's very difficult to raise them in the first few months. Your customers will resent the change, thinking you're either inexperienced or greedy. Bottom line—you lose more money than you gain if you raise your prices in the initial start-up.

The following is a list of some of the common expenses that are overlooked by beginners:

- Cost of permits
- Signage

- Deposits
- Operating capital
- Specialized software
- Service providers (accountants, attorneys, payroll, credit card service fees)
- Cleaning services
- Maintenance services
- Improvement and repair expenses
- Payroll taxes
- Costs of employee insurance and additional benefits like vacations and sick time

When planning your budget, separate your one-time start-up costs from your recurring monthly expenses to give you a true picture of regular monthly operating expenses. Of course, the problem is you may not realize what all those one-time costs will be until you start up. By then it could be too late to recover. Your best bet is to plan for all the expenses you know about and set aside a large lump sum for those you don't.

Chapter Two—Finding The Best And Training The Rest

Before you can hire the best, you need to have a vision of what type of person would work the best for your business. There are documents you'll need to create that will help you form that vision, and give you a hiring platform. Once you set a standard of excellence you can easily inform your candidates of the type of worker you're looking for and they'll know whether they'll be a good match for you as well. I mentioned helpful documents, so here's a few that will begin to create that picture for you.

Job Descriptions

There are as many job descriptions as there are jobs, and each one contains general and specific information that your new hire will need to know in order to perform to your expectations or industry standards. By creating a clear, well-written, and thorough job description ahead of time, you'll be able to more accurately hire someone who is a good fit for you and your company.

Although these are only the minimum elements needed for an efficient job description, it will at least help you to begin creating an image of that perfect candidate. Every job description should contain the following:

- Job title and position (formal and working titles)

- General summary of position (a few paragraphs that will be used to attract the best people for that position—make it position specific)
- Detailed description of job's duties (what is expected of the new hire)
- Standards (how will you expect the new hire to perform)
- Requirements (usually the minimum requirements needed to perform job)
- Pay range (be sure to give the range, not just one figure—this gives you room to vary pay based on experience and/or education)
- Direct contact person (include contact information)

Job descriptions don't need to be formal, but you should use complete sentences and make them position specific, truthful, and complete so that over or under qualified candidates don't waste their time and yours by applying for a job they don't want or are not qualified to perform. As you write your job descriptions, use action verbs and avoid vague language that could confuse or eliminate potential candidates. Some of the action verbs are:

Develop	**Establish**	**Evaluate**	**Guide**
Teach	Assign	Prepare	Solve
Verify	Observe	Complete	Lift
Update	Demonstrate	Initiate	Draft

The vague words that you'll want to avoid in your job descriptions include words like:

Sometimes   Frequently   Rarely   Maybe

These are words that are difficult to measure and do not work well when attempting to establish a certain standard or expectation. Think about it; one person may believe frequently means once a day while another person's frequent is once a week. To be fair to everyone, use words that convey specifics so all new hires are working on an even playing field.

Policy and Procedural Manual

You may have heard this called an employee handbook or new hire handbook. Whatever you choose to call it, there is legal information that is required by your state to be included. Every state has different requirements, so do your homework before printing your handbook. You may even decide to save yourself the cost and make it available on line so you can avoid the printing fees. Online manuals are usually much easier to access and refer to when employees need additional information.

Effective employee handbooks or guides should be written a little more vaguely so as not to lock you into specific directives that are known to frequently change. Most policy and procedural manuals will include the following information:

- About the company (mission and value statements and company history)

- Legalities about the employer's and employee's responsibilities to one another
- Ethical conduct and behaviors that are not necessarily legal requirements but rather reflect the company's culture
- Policies that share information about disciplinary actions, expected attendance, vacation time, and grounds for termination or remedies should the employee choose to be noncompliant
- Company benefits, such as paid time off, sick/personal days allowed, health care programs, insurance, etc...

This type of manual doesn't have to be formal but should always convey your expectations of the new hire and what they can expect of you as an employer. A well-written policy and procedural manual should empower your people by informing them of their rights.

90-Day Trial Agreements/Employment Agreements

Consider this to be more of a promise. Your new hire promises to give you're their best, and you do the same in exchange for the agreed upon pay. Many employers use a 90-day Trial Agreement in order to be clear about when they will and will not offer unemployment benefits if that new hire should quit or be terminated. I always felt the 90-day Trial Agreement was a "cover your back" type of document for employers.

Standard templates for each can be found online, but if you find there is a good deal of movement within your company, you may want to design a more company specific agreement that is better suited to your policy and procedural manual. The 90-day Trial Agreement should not be confused with an employment agreement. In fact, avoid using the word employment anywhere in your 90-day Trial Agreements because they specifically state that this is not an agreement to hire and that candidates should not consider themselves employees until being reviewed after the 90-day trial period.

Employment Application

These are quite common and ask for contact, employment history, educational background, career achievements, references, and tax exempt information. It's like an introduction interview on paper. If you have an accountant or payroll company, they may be able to share an employment packet with you that includes a standard application.

Waivers and Disclaimers

Your business may require the use of disclaimers or waivers that are distributed to certain customers. These agreements are usually those CYA (cover your ass) documents that protect both the employer and employee from those things for which customers might try to hold them liable. A word of warning, even when you have customers sign a waiver stating they will not hold you liable, it will not be worth the paper it's written on if they can prove you were negligent. For example, one of my associates owned an equestrian facility where she had all her borders and visiting riders sign a waiver which indemnified her of any responsibility. They agreed to follow the safety rules of the facility, wearing helmets and appropriate gear. However, one of the riders was injured in her arena, was not wearing a helmet, and was still able to hold the company liable. Waivers and disclaimers can be effective when people do not press the issue thinking they signed their rights away, but in this litigious society people can sue over almost anything. So beware!

Non-disclosures and Non-competes

These are also difficult to remedy should your employee choose to share information they shouldn't. Of course, if they are still working in your company, you can always fire them. However, if they have left your company and taken your knowledge and information with them, good luck. Even company specific intellectual properties that are illegally shared are near to impossible to prosecute. Besides, once the secret information is shared, it's just not a secret any longer now, is it?

All this talk about employers and employees, and you may not have even decided whether or not you're going to have employees. Your company may lend itself to hiring on a more temporary basis, such as day laborers and independent contractors. While it sounds great on the part of an employer because you can avoid payroll taxes on these types of workers, you may be in dangerous territory. I once knew a small business owner who decided to do just that: hire independent contractors instead of employees to avoid paying thousands of dollars each month in payroll taxes. She skated by for the first three years, but then the bomb dropped. A disgruntled independent contractor placed a formal complaint with the Department of Economic Security. The next thing the business owner knew, she was audited and fined thousands of dollars. She also had to pay back all the payroll taxes for the previous three years. What she thought was going to save her a little money each month ended up causing her to fold up shop because she simply couldn't pay the fines and back taxes.

The lesson to be learned here is that if you are considering whether or not to make your new hires employees or independent contractors, research the legalities of each. Your type of business may not qualify for independent contractors. Also, ask an accountant about how to legally deduct all you spend in day labor. In the end, it may be a wiser decision to simply hire.

Another expensive lesson for me was my mistaken belief about what qualified an employee to collect unemployment benefits. I had hired a gentleman, and I use that term loosely, whose performance was less than desirable and his attitude was even worse. I had no 90-day agreement, no employment agreement, just a hand-shake and a start date. After months of undocumented warnings, I finally decided I wanted him to be gone, but I was afraid to fire him because I thought he would file for unemployment.

One of my business associates advised me to cut his hours until he was forced to find other employment, so he would quit. Employees who quit couldn't collect unemployment, right? Wrong! Big mistake! The laws are usually written on the side of the employee. He was able to collect unemployment because his employment conditions had drastically changed and he could no longer work under the new conditions. I paid and he gloated.

I learned the hard way to consult an attorney, accountant, or the appropriate government agency about employee and employer rights. If I had known his and my rights, I could have avoided paying unemployment based on poor performance and insubordination. Instead, I tried to circumvent the system. Bad move on my part, but I did learn an invaluable lesson—do things fairly and legally and when you don't know the law—ask, ask, ask questions of those who do. Be smart about who you ask as well. Unless your neighbor or best friend is an attorney or judge, they're probably not going to know the answers.

Assuming you've created all your documents and done your homework before beginning the hiring process, now you're ready to interview but where are all the qualified candidates?

Hanging a sign in your storefront won't necessarily attract the best of the best. Placing ads in newspapers, online, or with employment services may not either. While all those methods help, one of the best ways to find the best people is to just go out there and steal them. You heard me—steal them!

It's common practice—every good business leader steals top producers from their competitors. You may want to think twice about walking into their place of business and announcing over the intercom that you have a better place to work for the top 5 percent of their employees. That might be a bit disturbing. However, there are good ways to steal good people. If you've been in business for any length of time, it's probably happened to you. Either a recruiter has attempted to persuade you to jump ship and come to the competitors, or someone has tried to steal one of your top producers. So, how do you protect yourself from such thievery?

The best way to keep your outstanding workers is to treat them well and pay them handsomely. Establish an unbeatable reputation of being the best company in town to work for, and you won't need to do much recruiting. Make it a privilege to work for your company, be known for hiring the elite, and you will attract the best of the best—in customers and employees.

The challenge for new businesses is that you have no proven track record. You have to be a good fisherman—casting your nets to capture a wide base of workers, and then throw back the ones who are not qualified or don't meet your standards. The throwbacks can often become the perfect workers though, and that's when you have to decide when to invest money in their training and when to count your losses and back away. You may put in all the time, effort, and money training an employee with great potential only to have them stolen by your competitor.

I once heard a businessman say he protected the investment he made in potentially great employees by treating them like he did his cell phone. When I asked him what he meant by that, he said he watched over them and always knew where they were at—just like his cell phone. He kept them close to his side and made them feel important—just like his cell phone. He trusted them with important information—just like his cell phone. They knew people who were as hard working and smart as they were, so he used them for contacts—just like his cell phone. If he did lose them to another company he tried everything to get them back—just like his cell phone. I think he's onto something here, don't you?

This brings me to my next point—where do you find the best of the best? This is when you apply the like attracts like rule. Hard workers, loyal workers, responsible workers, smart workers, usually hang with people who are very similar to them.   Hard working people don't normally associate with slugs, and should they have a friend or relative who is a slug they would never consider recommending them for a job. Ask your best workers who they know who would be a great worker just like they are. Make sure you create a substantial payoff for their recommendation. I promise the benefit you get from gaining another great employee will far outweigh the bonus or payoff you make to your employee.

Your choices are not just stealing or making a large payoff to attract the best of the best, you can also look for them within your industry or in related fields. Look out of state, participate in trade forums and paneled seminars, attend trade shows and spread the word that you're on the hunt. Be sure to let them know how picky you are about hiring the best people, though. Build your reputation as the best and people will perceive you that way. As a last resort, you may decide to hire the old way, through the classifieds. If you use these methods, don't forget to include the classifieds' online services.

Once you're ready to begin the interviewing process, be sure you understand the questions you can legally ask and those you cannot. For example, you cannot ask a woman of child-bearing age if she plans on having a child within the next few years. That could be considered discrimination. What you can do is have a relaxed conversation with them and talk about your family or some of the things your children do. Get them to share stories about their families, and before anyone is the wiser you'll add something like how you wouldn't want to be raising more children in this day and age, and observe their reaction. They may not say a word, but their facial expressions can give you a wealth of information.

Keeping an interview light and casual can gain you much more information than hard question after hard question that hammers the candidate and makes you head for happy hour. Almost every employer understands they cannot discriminate for age, race, sex preference, gender, religion, etc... However, what you may not totally understand is how your interviewing questions could be interpreted as discriminating ones. If you ask someone if they prefer Sundays off to attend church, you could be discriminating against those who are atheist. The best practice is to know the information you need to have to determine the best candidate and conduct a planned but casual conversation designed to legally reveal the candidates true beliefs and feelings. That's a mouthful, isn't it!

The interviewing process is not a crapshoot or random meeting in hopes that you'll magically identify the perfect candidate. It's a process, a hiring expedition and exploration that, if you're effective, can uncover and reveal those with innovative ideas and fresh enthusiasm for the job. Watching how a candidate responds to information provided can be just as informative or even more so than the words they speak. Facial expressions are most often spontaneous and truthful. For instance, asking a candidate if they do drugs most likely isn't going to get you to the truth. However, if you inform them that your company requires their employees to comply with random drug testing, that may be the end of that. You don't have to actually do random drug testing, just tell them you do—it's random. Keep in mind, it can be considered discrimination if you randomly test one employee but not another. If you're going to incorporate this practice, do it fairly.

Chapter Three—Advertising Angles and Marketing Momentum

We've all heard business owners say that the best advertising is word of mouth. That is a fact, but if you don't have customers to begin with—there's nobody doing the telling. I decided to group advertising and marketing together because most small business owners think of them as two of the same anyway, although each has a specific function. Marketing is identifying your potential type of customer. Will they be young and edgy, or older and more conservative?

What kind of spending habits do they have? Are they married, single, retirees, or students?

What colors, logos, branding, products, and services will attract your targeted customer? For example, if your best potential customer is a retiree with earnings of over $100,000 per year, you might want to avoid advertising picturing a 22-year-old youngster sitting in a red Corvette. That's definitely not going to be someone with whom they can identify. On the other hand, if you're trying to reach the young and upcoming entrepreneurs, you're not going to want to create advertising focused on gray beards lounging lakeside. Oh, if only your ideal customers were always this easy to identify.

You may not really know who your ideal customers would be, my friend sure didn't in her last business. She opened up a pet grooming salon and decided to work with a marketing agency to help her have a successful start-up.

One of the first questions they asked was who she felt was her ideal customer. She laughed and responded by saying her customer was anybody with a pet. In reality, she wouldn't have wanted just any old person with a pet. Did she really want to be grooming dogs and cats who hadn't been groomed for years and were matted to the hilt? Did she want the type of customer whose main focus was the price of the groom? Did she want customers who hopped from one groomer to the next, using the coupon of the month? Or, was she really looking for owners with mostly small pets needing regular grooming services who weren't adverse to paying a little more money for great products and excellent grooms? That's the one! Those were the customers she was looking to attract.

They then analyzed the location of her pet spa, and discovered she was smack dab between an upper-end, gated retirement community and a working middle-class residential area. Although there were thousands of other nearby residents not fitting these descriptions, she couldn't appeal to them all so she tried the retirees first. Her colors and logo were somewhat conservative; her slogan was solid and showed integrity and old-fashioned values. It worked! She did capture many of the other nearby residents as well, but her bread and butter business is still those retirees she marketed to when first building her business.

The challenges she experienced however were in her advertising. Most of the inexpensive advertising she could have done online was useless to attract retirees because few of them had or used computers. Facebook, Twitter, Linked-in, Yelp, Craigslist, and the rest were like a foreign language to those she had identified as her target market. She felt she had no other choice but to spend a lot of money on newspaper print ads and local magazines for high-dollar ads.

Fortunately, the more you search for inexpensive ways to advertise, the more success you're going to have. She discovered the retirement community had a local newspaper that was very inexpensive for small business advertising. She ran heavy discounts, but one of the smart things she did was make the discounts specific to the early morning hours. She knew other markets weren't known for early risers, and the retirees liked to get their chores done in the early morning. So, her marketing allowed her to identify the customer and her advertising opened up a whole new horizon by allowing them before opening hour appointments, by appointment only, where their dogs would only be with other small fluffy varieties like their own. What a hit that was; now they didn't have to fear little fluffy getting attacked by Bruno the boxer. Great strategy!

There is a step-by-step process to create marketing momentum and design advertising angles that work. Marketing always comes first. Avoid creating all your branding materials before you have truly identified your customer. This is another case where the customer comes first. Here are five easy steps to creating marketing momentum.

1. Identify your ideal customer
2. Research that customer base in your community
3. Find a marketing company whose clients deal with the same type customer
4. Know your competition and decide how you will be unique and different—set yourself apart
5. Design your branding and marketing materials around your desired customer and focus on what makes your company unique and different

Now move to the advertising angles you will apply. Here are five easy steps to planning special advertising angles that will let your customers know what you do.

1. Research where your ideal customers are currently going and what products and services they purchase.

2. Discover what types of advertising best reaches your desired customer, and begin with the advertising that is least expensive.

3. Make it a habit to market to less people more frequently rather than more people less frequently. Repetition is crucial when building your customer base.

4. Advertise your differences and their added value. Avoid advertising lowest price unless your ideal customer is a bargain shopper

5. Don't depend on only one kind of advertising. Try different types of advertising, like print, social media, TV/radio, direct mail, etc. Be sure to

track your advertising dollars in order to determine what works best.

Plan a huge and very "Grand" opening. No matter what the age or income of your desired customer, everybody loves a party. Make it fun and profitable—exciting and interactive. One of my associates had a great turnout for his grand opening by floating balloons on the ceiling and placing coupons for products inside the balloons. The catch was, three of the balloons had $500 in cash inside. It's true, he forfeited $1,500, but the customers he gained who purchased with their coupons and were also returning customers far outweighed the $1,500 giveaway.

Food is another item that should be on your list when planning great "Grand" openings. If it's possible, cook outside and let everybody smell your opening extravaganza. Cook out hamburgers and hotdogs, and get the media to participate. Most local papers have a new business section.   Have them announce the opening of your business and your "Grand" opening in that new business section.

The most important thing to remember is to plan for success.   I don't care if you have to pull in neighbors, family, and people off the street— have plenty of help to serve all the new customers your grand opening will attract. Make it remarkable.   Get people talking about you, your company, your products and services, and your helpful staff.   If the surrounding communities have community blogs, contact a current customer who lives in the community and ask them to talk you up on their blog. Make sure you show your appreciation for their help.

There are hundreds of ways to advertise—some are outrageous, some conservative, some cost a fortune, some make you a fortune.   The important thing is that you do it. Don't just sit behind your desk and wait for the customers to come to you. Get out there and serve your community. Show them you've got what they want, and you're willing to work with them to make sure they get it for a fair price in good time with nice people.

Chapter Four—Your Customer Return Policy

This is not about returning products or money back for perceived poor service. That's not what I mean when I say customer return policy. What I'm talking about is how often will your customers come back and what do you plan to do to get them returning more often with larger purchases? That's your Customer Return Policy. Let's discuss the types of consumers within your customer base.

The "Spoil Me" Customer

These are people who love being pampered. They love it when you make them feel special and give them a little goodie here and there. They are the people who love samples and treats, so keep some on hand just for them. You may even want to keep some of these behind the desk and make it seem as though you were waiting for them to come in and picked these up just for them.

The Royalty Customer

These are people who think they're better than everybody else—more important, more deserving. They usually drive fancy cars and wear expensive jewelry, and they like it to be noticed and fussed over. Then they brush it off, pretending to be embarrassed that you noticed. They will expect you to follow behind them to fold or put away discarded items. They like to purchase the most expensive items and let others know how much they spent. The good thing is, they'll send you customers just like they are, and you'll have an entire base of clients who try to top one another's spending. A word of caution! They like to gossip about each other as well, so avoid that trap.

The "Know My Name" Customer

These are people who like to be called by name. They like being remembered, so keep a database with notes on your people. Key into something about them that will help you remember their name. The next time they visit your store ask them about something that was concerning them the time before. They'll appreciate your concern. Use their name when they first walk in and call them by name when they leave. It could be as simple as a "See you next time, Bill. Tell Doris (wife) I missed her."

The Special Service Customer

These are people who always ask for something special. If you are selling food, they want to sample everything before making their decision. If you are providing a printing service, they want a flyer designed free and then they'll pay for the printing. They can be demanding and annoying, but once you have convinced them you are the best, they're loyal and appreciative. You will recognize these types of customers right away, because they will tell you about all the free stuff your competitors gave them.

The Needy Customer

These are people who always have a problem that needs immediate attention. They will suck up your time with question after question about some imagined problem or concern. They are difficult to deal with when you are busy or having a particularly challenging issue that needs your attention as well. And, they usually don't like being passed off to one of your staff members. They want to be served by the owner or manager.

These are people who make up the toothpick brigade. They wander around the store with a toothpick in their mouths, lifting up this and playing with that. They ask questions about everything, but they rarely pull the trigger on a purchase. They sample everything, but never buy. Their favorite phrase is "Oh, I love that." But, before you know it they're putting it down and moving on to something else they won't buy. These types of customers can get all the way to checkout, change their minds, and leave the cartful of merchandise to be put away by your staff. Most of the time, you'll have to straighten the entire store when they leave.

The Never Satisfied Customer

These are people who, no matter what you do, can never be satisfied. The more you offer, the more they complain. The best thing to do with these types of customers is simply to listen and validate them. You don't really have to give them anything, just understand and commiserate with their dissatisfaction. In fact, no matter what you try to do to please them, they're going to leave just like they came in—unhappy.

The Impulsive Customer

These people are those who begin picking up merchandise you have displayed outside. They'll even pick up your phone thinking it's something they can purchase. The fuller their basket, the better they feel. The problem with these types of customers is that they rush to purchase unneeded items, and then they'll bring them back the next day and want a refund. They can cause your staff a lot more work to reshelf items and write return tickets.

The Search and Conquer Customer

These people have a mission in mind when they come into your store to buy. They know what they want, and they don't appreciate being up sold. They just want to find the item and get back home. They don't care about the sales, discounts, or new products, and if you try to tell them about all those things—they'll cut you off. They can be abrupt and borderline rude, so give them exactly what they ask for and rush them to checkout.

Not all customers fall into these specific categories. Some are no fuss no muss customers who are pleasant and love to offer insightful suggestions that will help you build your business. They are eager and pleasant and fun to serve, and they show their appreciation by returning again and again to purchase your goods and services. They too recommend other customers who are just like they are, so treat them well and you'll soon find that you have created a business that caters to wonderful customers.

Chapter Five—Weathering the Storms

You've done everything right, and yet you're still having a hard time? Welcome to the world of business ownership. If it were easy, everybody would own a business and make a million. You can count on there being some rough spots here and there; even the most successful entrepreneurs experience them. If it's any comfort to you, you're in good company.

There are many reasons why entrepreneurs fail in the beginning, or even well beyond their first few successes. Not all of the storms these owners and their companies weathered were due to financial challenges. Henry Ford closed shop because he couldn't get along with his business partner. Google has probably experienced more epic failures than any other hugely successful company, and yet they are one of today's most popular computer tools. Why has Google not succumbed to the myriad of failures they've produced? Along with their epic failures, they continued to innovate and have unbeatable successes—Google Chrome, for example. The key to Google's success has been they continue to innovate, to celebrate the failures that have lead them to huge successes. When their video player failed, they didn't just throw up their hands, whine, or deny it. Knowing the value of their idea, they simply pursued a different avenue. They bought YouTube. There are lessons to be learned from

Google's failures. If you know you have a good idea, but your design is flawed—search out another avenue.

The truth is, the more creative and innovative you are, the more likely you are to experience failure. On the flip side, innovation and creativity can also create successes that far exceed your failures. Many companies and entrepreneurs who succeed do so because they were able to pull themselves up after every catastrophic failure, learn from their mistakes, and continue on their quest for success.

Another common problem can occur at the other end of the spectrum—some people stop creating and innovating after they have experienced a huge success. Big mistake! Another thing you can always count on is somebody else capitalizing on your successes. They'll take your idea, improve or update it, and the fickle public will go with the latest and greatest play on your initial success. Even though one or two sizeable successes have kept you well ahead of your competition, avoid the temptation to set back and ride it out. One or two successes will not see you through a lifetime. It takes a lifetime of successes to ride out the storms.

Riding out the storms are easier said than done, that's for sure—especially when you've been hit by one failure after another and your associates and family are feeling sorry for you. Your loved ones may mean well, but pity is definitely not going to push you to greater achievements. When those you love encourage you to quit, it takes a determined business person to hold the line, to search for another answer, to throw more money and time into something that everybody else believes is a failure. This is when the champions dig in and dig out of the giant holes in the confidence created by repeated failures. It's easy to be confident when you're enjoying a successful business, but quite the other story when your failures are so public everybody offers you sympathy and asks what you're going to do now.

What is also so perverse is that your business can be on the brink of going under, and your competitors are enjoying the most profitable year they've ever had. It never fails, and it can be so disheartening. Keep in mind, though, this may be their time to shine, but there is another truth in business. On the heels of great success nip the hungry dogs of failure. I don't care how successful your competitors are, if they also don't continue to innovate and create and you do, you'll leave them in your dust. Following are my "List of Six Steps to Success."

1. Plan for the worst but expect the best. In other words, don't bleed your company of funds in the good times. Instead, set some aside to continue operations when you're experiencing the storms.

2. Advertise and market all the time—in good times and in bad. What a temptation it is to stop your marketing and advertising when business is booming and you don't think you need to advertise or market any longer. Not to mention the difficulties of spending money you don't have on advertising and marketing when your business is down. Limiting your budget for these things will doom your business. Don't stop advertising and marketing, find ways to actually increase your marketing and stretch your advertising dollars. Look to online ventures, they are your best bet for inexpensive marketing and advertising.

3. Continue creating and innovating. Avoid celebrating your successes or lamenting your losses for too long. Either way you're not moving forward. Business never remains static. If you aren't progressing, moving forward, you're

losing ground to your competitors who are.

4. Have faith in yourself and your dream of building a business. Refuse to listen to those naysayers who drag you down with their negatives. Here's a moto that's good to live by. If people don't leave you feeling better about yourself and your business plans—don't include them in your plans. Avoid talking to them about your next endeavor, about how you're going to apply this failure to a new and better idea that you believe will bring you success. Even if those who are pulling you down are loved ones, when times are bad only share your ideas with those who believe in you and your ability to achieve success.

5. Be determined and persistent on your path to success. The farther you let failure pull you to the side of your dream, the more you'll muddle in the mud at the

side of the road and finally be forever stuck in the mire of your own discouragement. If you have properly planned for failure while dreaming of success, you'll be able to come through to the other side with more knowledge and a greater chance for future success. Every failure is an opportunity to learn, getting you one step closer to your dream. Hold your head high; there is no shame in failure, only in not trying.

6. Don't be afraid to admit you're in trouble and ask other experts in your field for help. Ask for help from your loyal customers. It has always amazed me how many wonderful ideas your best consumers can have. However, few will ever share those ideas with you unless you ask. If you provide a service, some of your best customers may have always wished they could find someone who would do this or that. They're a source of

great ideas you may never have thought to tap until you're right in the middle of a storm. You don't have to wait for the bad times; ask good customers for their input all the time. Have a suggestion box and reward them for their contributions. Great successes are born from simple suggestions. Who knows? One of your customer's expressed needs could be your next great success.

Another untapped source of creativity may be in your staff. They work in your business as much if not more than you. They are your front line, the face of your company. They see things that you do not, and perhaps have ideas that you haven't considered. Value what your staff has to say and encourage their participation in the inside workings of your business. As always, recognize their contributions and celebrate their creativity.

Chapter Six—Think Big

Think like the big boys—think big. If you are always consumed by the small stuff, that's exactly what you'll be producing and creating— small stuff. Thinking big will enable you to do business differently and give you the edge over your competition. Thinking big lets you be distinctive, remarkable, bigger and better. Plan to outgrow your storefront before you ever get into it. Now that's thinking big. Explore how you can expand your business to other nearby locations, preferably right next door. If you are considering a space, avoid sandwiching yourself between two other businesses. Give yourself room to expand into the space next door. Your landlord could get a new tenant before you're ready to expand, but it never hurts to plan ahead. If you are willing to take two spaces at once, your landlord will more than likely give you a substantial break on your monthly lease and build-outs.

If you have already leased a spot that does not allow for growth, then the next best thing is to start gobbling up your nearby competition. Investigate public records and see who has been in their space for three to five years. Approach the owner and ask if he or she might be interested in entertaining an offer to purchase their business. Let them know that you are so busy you're needing to expand. It never hurts to let your competitors know you're doing great and are going to threaten their business anyway. You may want to tell them that rumor has it they are looking to get out of the business. So you're fudging a bit. Who knows, it may be the truth.

Guaranteed, the business you wish to purchase may give you a first number that is astronomical; everybody over-estimates the value of their business. Do your homework; be prepared with a reasonable and fair number that you believe their business is worth. Be polite, and come with proof of your numbers. Let them know how you are offering more value for your customers, like using higher-end products or providing more customized services. You don't have to brag about it, though. In fact, make it sound as though you are almost complaining about it. Say something like, "It's amazing how our industry has changed. What used to be going the extra mile yesterday is what most customers expect today. I can't believe how much more it is costing me to serve the same customers this year as compared to last year. It sure makes it difficult for us small business owners, doesn't it?"

When you talk about what customers expect today, make sure it is the very thing that makes you different—something that you provide and they do not. That will get them thinking about what they are going to need to invest just to keep up. They may consider the fact that this would be a great time to sell and retire or move on. Statistics show that 80 percent of businesses between 3 and 5 years fold, so take advantage of that number and approach your competitors within that time frame.

If your competitor is doing far more business than you are, you may also want to consider merging. Take a calculated risk. With two big thinkers, you just may corner the market. What's the worst that could happen? Your competitor says "no." No problem. Or, you look at his figures and can't make the numbers work—no problem. At least you'll have a better understanding of where you stand.

Something else to consider is that this might be the perfect time for you to sell. Thinking big may mean making a bold move into another business. If your numbers have been static for over a year, you may have reached your peak. Or, you may need to think of other avenues to create additional revenue.   Either way, it requires thinking big. It may not be time to sell at all, but rather time to open another location. If this is something you want to toss around, make sure your original location can stand alone and actually support a new one for a while. If not, you'll be in danger of starving one location to feed another. You will also be dividing your time between the two locations unless you have dynamite help, so consider the demands this move may make on your time.

Thinking big may not mean any of the above, but it may still mean being a risk taker. What if you were to raise your prices? What would that do for your business? Some people live in fear that raising their prices will make their customers mad, and they'll take their business elsewhere. That may be true for those customers who are coming to you because you're the lowest in town. However, if you have marketed your business as upper-end, catering to the elite, they will be fine with a small increase. Always keep in mind, when you raise your prices give your customers some added value and let them know about it. If you have always used the best products but never made a big deal of it, now's the time. Let them know that you use the very best products on the market. If you offer regular hours that are also common to your nearby competition, make it more convenient for your customers to come to your business.

Think of it as a tradeoff. You're trading a little higher price for a lot more service and/or better product. When you are presenting this to your customers, only talk about the amount you have raised—not the entire amount for your product or service. For example, if your average sale is $50, and you're going to raise it to $55. Don't get pulled into a discussion of why your product or service is $55. Minimize it by saying, I know you appreciate the best, and for just $5 more, you are getting (then name all they are getting for that price—even if they had already been getting it for the original $50.) Minimize price—maximize value.

If selling is on your mind, think big. What would it take for you to walk? What would you do if you weren't in this business any longer? If you've learned how to think big, your brain is already spinning out a new business venture and how to build that one. Whatever you decide to do, do it BIG!

Conclusion—Practice the ABCs of Business

Your business ABCs are to (Always Be Creating). If you constantly think about what you're going to do next, there will always be a next. Whether it's the next step in this business, or the next new business to build to a great success, you will be stepping up your business. Once you have learned how to build a successful first business, the second one is a piece of cake. It could be a totally different industry, but the methods of building a business remain the same. The strategies are the same, and so are the ABCs. It is absolutely imperative that you ALWAYS BE CREATING. Create a great business for yourself. Create happiness. Create fun and joy in your work. Create financial freedom. Create a business that runs itself and allows you to semi-retire. Create a new way to do an old business. That's what it's all about—creating.

The most important thing to create is a great reputation in your business. Be known for integrity, impeccable service, and caring workers. Do this and you will soon own the community you serve. Whenever you get new customers in your store, ask them where they were going before and what they loved about the place. Don't ever speak harshly of your competition; it's in very bad taste. Besides, knowing what they are doing right can get you much further. If you aren't doing what your new customer loves, explain to them how you have taken it one step further. If you need to be doing what your new customer loves, tell them you love that idea too and you're going to incorporate it into your service or product. If it is something you wouldn't think of doing because you believe it's bad policy, change the subject and let them know you have something they'll love even more. Remember, there is a reason that customer has left the old place and searched for a new one in which to bring their business.

Don't talk like a "topper," if you know what I mean. In other words, if someone says their previous place did such and such and you know you do it better, don't sound like a braggart. Don't word it this way: "Oh, we do it much better than they do. That's what we did years ago." Be a professional. Say it this way: "Oh, I thought that was a great idea as well when I first started my business. After using that method for a while, we found that doing it this way (explanation) gave our customers (name the benefits to the customer). Speaking in this manner will allow you to share your big ideas, practice your ABCs, and do so in a positive and professional manner.

Start today to use these methods and build your business beyond what you thought yesterday would have been its maximum potential. Now you have a greater understanding and know differently about the best way to build, right? After reading this book, you'll broaden your horizons—think bigger and perform better. You'll recognize the approaching storms and be prepared to face them head-on with your head up. Make a decision today to build a business that challenges you and brings you joy and satisfaction. My dad once told me "If it's not fun, it won't get done." That is so true when it comes to building a business. If that business becomes a burden to you, it's really not worth the effort.

Build a business that builds confidence, builds satisfaction, builds financial freedom, and builds a success cycle that is second to none.

www.ingramcontent.com/pod-product-compliance
Lightning Source LLC
Chambersburg PA
CBHW041103180526
45172CB00001B/93